The Only Way is Ethics

QUILTBAG

Jesus and sexuality

Sean Doherty

T0326057

First published 2015 by Authentic Media Limited,
52 Presley Way, Crownhill, Milton Keynes, MK8 0ES.
authenticmedia.co.uk

British Library Cataloguing in Publication Data
A catalogue record for this book is available from the British Library.
ISBN: 978-1-78078-146-4   978-1-78078-435-9 (e-book)

Cover design by Sara Garcia

QUILTBAG – Queer, Undecided, Intersex, Lesbian, Trans-sexual, Bisexual, Asexual, Gay.

What is sexuality?

Terms such as homosexual, heterosexual and bisexual are relatively new. I recently read a book, translated in the mid-1980s, that used the word 'sexuality' to mean that human beings are male and female. Being sexual meant being a physical sex, female or male. Today, 'sexuality' denotes 'sexual orientation' – whether gay, straight, or something else.

Most people today assume that sexuality is something real and definite. You simply are straight, or gay, or bi. Gay people don't choose to be gay any more than straight people choose to be straight. A shorthand for this view is 'essentialism', because it holds that sexuality is an essential part of you. We can even look back through history and identify gay individuals from the past, because we assume that their experience and reality of being gay then is pretty much the same as it is now, though of course far less understood then. The idea that we understand sexuality much better now than in the past massively heightens the pressure on the church to change its view of sexual morality. I have had conversations with people who regard me as blinded by my faith from accepting the 'clear' findings of science concerning sexuality. Our culture tends to assume that it is not our experience of sexuality that is new (people have always been gay, straight, bi and so on), but our improved understanding of it.

I think that essentialism is very simplistic about what 'science' says about sexuality. There has been excellent and insightful research on sexuality, but note two things about that research. First, we need a lot more. There are many things we still don't know, such as what causes sexual orientation. Genetics? Upbringing? A complex mix of different factors?[1] Second, some research actually undermines the essentialist view, suggesting that sexuality is a lot more complicated and diverse than we often assume.[2]

I also think that essentialism is historically simplistic. No doubt there has always been same-sex desire, activity and relationships. But what they have looked like has varied from culture to culture.[3] The ancient writers who wrote

------

[1]See the authoritative recent review of scientific research in this area by Eleanor Whiteway and Denis R. Alexander, 'Understanding the causes of same-sex attraction', in *Science and Christian Belief* (2015), 27, pp. 17–40, online at https://www.scienceandchristianbelief.org/serve_pdf_free.php? filename=SCB+27-1+Whiteway+Alexander.pdf, with additional material here https://www.scienceandchristianbelief.org/download_pdf_free.php? filename=Whiteway-long-version-ed.pdf.

[2]See Peter Ould, 'Can your sexuality change?' online at http://www.livingout.org/can-your-sexuality-change-, and Lisa Diamond, 'Just How Different are Female and Male Sexual Orientation?' a video lecture online at http://www.cornell.edu/video/lisa-diamond-on-sexual-fluidity-of-men-and-women.

[3]See Peter Ould, 'Surely the homosexual activity prohibited by the Bible was totally different to what we're familiar with today?' online at http://www.livingout.org/surely-the-homosexual-activity-prohibited-by-the-bible-was-totally-different-to-what-we-re-familiar-with-today-.

about same-sex relationships in their day were no less sophisticated and observant than us. So, if sexual orientation is universal and an essential part of human identity, I find it surprising that nobody realised this before – that we have an accurate self-knowledge they lacked.

This does not mean that sexual orientation is not real. It is. But it could well be more complicated, varying somewhat in understanding and experience by time and place. The context in which we find ourselves shapes our experience and understanding of ourselves, including our sexualities. So the main rival to essentialism is the theory that sexuality is (at least partly) socially constructed. (This can still include the view that there is something universal underneath the different social constructions, but experienced and understood differently in different cultures.) For example, Professor Sue Wilkinson, who was married (to a man) for seventeen years said, 'I was never unsure about my sexuality throughout my teens or twenties. I was a happy heterosexual and had no doubts. Then I changed, through political activity and feminism, spending time with women's organisations. It opened my mind to the possibility of a lesbian identity.'[4] What was significant for her was involvement in a community in which a new kind of identity became possible. Cultural and social factors may shape sexual identity, at least for some people.

At the radical end of this 'constructed' approach, some people even believe that there is an element of choice involved (although they do not necessarily deny the reality

---

[4] http://www.wnd.com/2007/07/42356/.

of sexual orientation).[5] Peter Tatchell, who has tirelessly campaigned against the mistreatment of gay people, often at great personal cost, has made some statements that come close to this approach, although he believes that biology is also a factor. For example, he asks, 'If we are all born either gay or straight, how do they explain people who switch in mid-life from fulfilled heterosexuality to fulfilled homosexuality (and vice versa)?'[6]

Similarly, at the more radical end of contemporary gender theory is the idea that we need to deconstruct male and female as fixed, opposite categories, because the very notion of gender is itself corrupt and patriarchal. If male and female do not actually exist as such, how can there be such a thing as sexual orientation?

Almost all of these approaches are onto something. Essentialists best describe how most people today become aware of their sexuality: as a given. Nobody wakes up one day with a completely blank slate and thinks, 'What sexuality shall I be?' Sexual orientation clearly isn't a free choice

---

[5]See http://www.queerbychoice.com/. Similarly, the journalist Matthew Parris has written, 'I think sexuality is a supple as well as subtle thing, and can sometimes be influenced, even promoted; I think that in some people some drives can be discouraged and others encouraged; I think some people can choose.' 'Are you gay or straight? Admit it, you are most likely an in-between.' *The Times* (5.8.2006).

[6]Peter Tatchell, 'Born gay or made gay?' *Guardian* (28.6.2006), online at http://www.theguardian.com/commentisfree/2006/jun/28/borngayormadegay. See also 'Future Sex: Beyond Gay and Straight', *Huffington Post* (9.1.2012), online at http://www.huffingtonpost.co.uk/peter-g-tatchell/sex-future-beyond-gay-and-straight_b_1195017.html.

in that sense. Indeed, some gay people admit that they would have chosen to be straight if they'd had a choice. It's not that they are ashamed of their sexuality – it's just that life would have been simpler and less painful in a world which is still not fully accepting towards them.

The social constructionists are also onto something in their recognition that society and culture play a major role in making us who we are. When I identified myself as gay, it was simply because that was the word provided for me by my world.

And the more radical 'choice' theorists are also onto something. They are right to recognise that, whilst most people have no choice when it comes to their sexual feelings, adopting a particular sexual identity involves an element of choice – and certainly sexual feelings can be influenced by our choices, although I am not saying that it is possible to change one's sexual orientation through choice.[7] I chose to stop identifying myself as gay, not because I had then experienced any change in my sexual feelings, but because I had come to believe that my sexual identity should be defined in terms of my physical gender and not in terms of my orientation.

As you'll have noticed in what I have just said, homosexuality is a real and personal issue for me. Elsewhere in this series, in *Living Out My Story*, I have shared my story and offered some thoughts about how the church

---

[7]For an excellent if older discussion of choice, see Edward Stein, *The Mismeasure of Desire: The Science, Theory, and Ethics of Sexual Orientation* (New York: Oxford University Press, 1999), ch. 9–10.

can truly welcome and care for gay people, without com-
promising what I have called the 'classic' Christian view
that sex is for marriage only, and that marriage is the union
of a woman and a man. In my experience, that conviction
was liberating and life-giving. What follows here sets out
the theological basis for it.

Understanding why the Bible and the church teach that sex is only for marriage

There has been an inordinate amount of ink spilled over
what the various biblical prohibitions of same-sex activity
mean. Some authors argue fiercely that these texts refer
to sex in a context of idolatry, slavery and paedophilia,
and therefore cannot possibly apply to loving, faithful,
consenting same-sex relationships today. But these
authors have not often engaged with the theological
and biblical reasons why the church has classically taught
that same-sex activity is prohibited. It is not enough to
say that the classic biblical 'proof texts' do not apply
to monogamous, faithful same-sex relationships. To
be convincing, this perspective needs to show that the
reasons for the prohibition no longer apply.

However, an equal weakness amongst those arguing
for the classic view, that sex is only for marriage and that
marriage is only between a woman and a man, has been
a lack of explanation as to why this is so. There's no point
keeping a rule unless there are good reasons for it – and
many people today can't see the point of this rule, no
matter what the texts actually say. Even worse, some pro-
ponents of the classic view try to give objectively verifiable

reasons for it in order to convince people that it is correct. For example, Christians have claimed that same-sex relationships are inherently less committed or faithful than opposite-sex ones, or that homosexual activity is physically dangerous, that gay people are more likely to develop sexually transmitted diseases, and so on. This approach makes the classic view sound homophobic to contemporary ears, and places itself at the mercy of the next empirical study. You can't use contextual evidence to prove what you are claiming is a universal moral viewpoint. For example, you could equally argue that same-sex relationships have only been less faithful precisely because they did not have the regulation and security of marriage.

So, it should be pretty clear that we need to look at the reasons behind the classic Christian view of sex and marriage, and we turn to this now.

Jesus, sex and marriage

The first and most important reason for the church's teaching is the teaching of Jesus himself. It is sometimes argued that because Jesus never directly mentioned same-sex relationships (or to be precise, that if he did then it is not recorded in the gospels), then the church has no business teaching about them either. But we cannot read too much into Jesus's silence. There are many things the gospels do not mention. They are not intended as an exhaustive rule book.

Given what the Old Testament says about same-sex activity (as we shall see) and the universal disapproval of it within the Judaism of Jesus's time, it would be surprising if Jesus underwent a radical rethink about the issue but never got round to mentioning it. After all, he frequently challenged received wisdom, and the gospels do not shy away from describing the controversies he caused. Jesus's radical love for all and inclusion and acceptance of outcasts did not stop him from saying that sin was sin (as in the famous example of John 8:11).[8]

More concretely, when Jesus was quizzed on a controversial issue of sexual morality within his day (divorce), he looks to the creation stories in Genesis 1 and 2 in order to discern God's intention for marriage and sex. This is why the church has always taken these stories as especially significant. So Jesus is quoting from Genesis when he says, 'God made them male and female' and 'a man shall leave his father and mother and hold fast to his wife, and they shall become one flesh' (Mark 10:7–8, and also Matt. 19:5). Jesus therefore defined and understood marriage as being the union of a woman and a man through sexual intercourse ('one flesh'), precisely because God made human beings female and male. If this was Jesus's view of marriage and the purpose of sex within it, it is difficult to see how we can interpret Jesus as supporting *any* sex outside marriage, including same-sex activity.

If Jesus turned to the creation stories in Genesis 1 and 2 in order to understand marriage and sex, and to resolve a controversial question of sexual morality, that is the best

---

[8]See John Nolland, 'Sexual Ethics and the Jesus of the Gospels', *Anvil* 26.1 (2009), online at http://www.biblicalstudies.org.uk/pdf/anvil/26-1_021.pdf.

model for us to follow also. In our attempt to understand why Scripture prohibits same-sex activity, we will now therefore look at these stories too.

Sexuality and the Trinity

What is the most important thing about God? When I teach on sexuality, I usually start with this question. Someone almost always replies, 'God is love,' to which I answer, 'Why? What makes God love?' That normally elicits silence. Other typical answers are, 'God is the Creator' or 'all-powerful'. All these answers are true, of course, but are they God's most important and fundamental reality? Sooner or later, we hit the answer. Here it is. The most important thing about God is: God is 'Triune'.

Triune is not a word we use regularly, although 'Trinity' is more familiar. Triune shows the original meaning of Trinity: three = one. Most Christians know, in theory at least, that God is somehow both three and one. That's why God is love. At God's deepest level, God is fundamentally relationship – three persons who are different (though equal), but in a relationship of such perfect love that they are one just as much as they are three. God really is three persons, yet there is only one God. Both the oneness and the threeness matter equally.

What has that to do with sex? Well, this relational, tripersonal God says, 'Let us make man in our image, after our likeness' (Gen. 1:26). Note the 'us' and 'our' – as if more than one person is speaking. Many Christian interpreters have read this as a reference to the Trinity, although this was not what it meant originally.[9] But it is striking that when a fundamentally relational God decides to create someone like God, to reflect and represent God in the world, God does it by making us male and female (v. 27).

So, being male and female, being sexual, is how we are like God, because God is fundamentally different persons in fundamental unity. Similarly, women and men are fundamentally different, yet fundamentally the same. Our common humanity unites us, as can the intimacy of sexual intercourse. As Christopher Roberts puts it, 'Marriage relies on two modes of being human that are utterly distinct and yet created for partnership.'[10] It is the genuine difference between women and men which reflects the real difference of persons in God. Yet, just as importantly, men and women are fundamentally the same, reflecting God's own unity. It is only together that we reflect God, and neither gender can reflect God on its own. (This is also why women and men are equal, just as Father, Son and Holy Spirit are equal.)

Following the example of Jesus, the Christian tradition has read these verses as a reference not only to our common humanity, but also to marriage. It would be easy to

---

[9]For fuller discussion of different possible interpretations, see for example Claus Westermann, *Genesis I–II: A Commentary*, trans. John J. Scullion (London: SPCK, 1984), p. 142ff.

[10]Christopher C. Roberts, *Creation and Covenant: The Significance of Sexual Difference in the Moral Theology of Marriage* (London: T & T Clark, 2007), p. 94. The whole book is a must-read if you want to explore this issue more deeply.

assume that only people who are like one another can get along. For example, some ancient writers believed that men could only truly be friends with other men. But in the Trinity, and in Genesis, difference does not hinder union, but enables it. It is precisely the difference between Father and Son which makes their relationship one of perfect fatherhood and sonship. And it is precisely the difference between women and men, including the physical genital difference, that enables them to be truly physically united into 'one flesh' through sexual intercourse (Genesis 2:18). We really can be united, without having to become the same. Indeed, we need to be different, if we are to be united.

Any supporter of same-sex activity from a Christian perspective must therefore answer a fundamental question: how can we regard the union of two people of the same sex as a 'one flesh' union in the sense of Genesis 2? It might well be a 'one heart' and 'one mind' union – but those things alone are not what make a marriage.

In summary, being women and men, i.e. sexually different, is the way humans reflect and are like God. Just as God is relational and interdependent, and not solitary, we too are relational at our most fundamental level. Sex is therefore a permanent, inherent feature of who we are, as we can see in the fact that Jesus's resurrected body is still male. In the new heaven and earth, physical life is not abolished, but reaffirmed and perfected. Therefore sexuality is fundamental to being human, even though having sex is not.[11]

---

[11] *Creation and Covenant*, p. 107.

Marriage and the relationship between Christ and the church

So, the first reason that being sexual creatures matters is that our unity-through-difference reflects God's. The New Testament adds a second reason: marriage is a picture of the gospel. Far from being prudish about marriage and sex, the Bible compares the relationship between God and humanity to sex. Just as wife and husband are fundamentally different, so are Jesus and the church.[12] Yet the wonder of the gospel is that, rather than Jesus remaining separated from the church by his greatness and our sin, he truly unites himself to us, bringing us salvation and wholeness. The gospel is not simply forgiveness (although it is), nor that we have a new relationship with God (although we do). The gospel is also union with Christ: we have been made one with Jesus, and thereby share his holiness and relationship to the Father.

Again, then, the difference between women and men in marriage cannot be downplayed. Our union with Christ doesn't make us the *same* as him. Me is not short for Messiah! Like a married couple, Jesus and his bride remain distinct people. Yet we are utterly made for each other and truly united. This is the reason why sex must be between people who are fundamentally (or ontologically) different to one another, as men and women are fundamentally different. Sex within marriage shows

---

[12]This image is used in Ephesians 5:23–33 and Revelation 19:6–9.

that people who are truly different can also be truly united (which is also why marriage must be a permanent union), and in this way sex is a picture of the gospel.

This means that sex must be between a man and a woman for exactly the same reason that it must be within the permanence of marriage. The point of sex is not simply to unite *any* two individuals, even if they love one another and are completely committed for life, but to embody the union between people who are fundamentally different. The Father, the Son and the Spirit are fundamentally different but perfectly one. Christ and the church are also different, yet truly united. God's good purpose for sex in creation is therefore to show that two fundamentally different people can be permanently and truly united. Anyone who wishes to argue that promiscuity and adultery are wrong but not same-sex activity, needs to show why this fundamental feature of the biblical picture of sex no longer applies, when the other features still do.

Isn't sex within marriage primarily about procreation?

One reason often offered for the classic view of sex advocated here is that procreation can only take place between a woman and a man. This is a very consistent view for Roman Catholics and others who believe that contraception is wrong. For them, sex and procreation cannot be separated. But an overemphasis on procreation is an own goal for people who believe that contraception is legitimate. If sex does not inherently have to be procreative, why restrict it to opposite-sex couples?[13]

It's true that procreation is emphasised in Genesis 1. God blesses humanity and tells them to 'Be fruitful and multiply and fill the earth and subdue it' (v. 28). But this is a general instruction to humanity as a whole, not necessarily an obligation on every married couple. Just as this command does not oblige everyone to marry in the first place, it does not oblige every married couple to procreate. A small minority of couples may choose to remain childless for selfish reasons. But there can also be very good reasons for a couple to remain childless, such as if they are both carriers of a genetic disease or because of mental health concerns. And there are many marriages that are childless through infertility or because they took place after childbearing age. Such marriages are no less valid or good, even without (humanly speaking) the prospect of procreation. Similarly, there are many sexual acts that have the potential for procreation but are not right and natural, such as casual sex, rape and adultery. There is more to marriage than procreation.

Genesis 2 makes no mention of procreation at all. The creation of the woman happens because, as God announces, 'It is not good that the man should be alone' (Gen. 2:18). None of the animals corresponds to the man sexually or in terms of companionship and intimacy. But

---

[13]This is essentially the argument made by Robert Song in *Covenant and Calling: Towards a Theology of Same-Sex Relationships* (London: SCM, 2014).

the woman does, as the man recognises when God presents her to him:

> 'This at last is bone of my bones
> and flesh of my flesh;
> she shall be called Woman,
> for she was taken out of Man.'
>
> *Genesis 2:23*

This isn't just biology – it's chemistry! Woman is like man: formed from his very bone and flesh. Yet she is also different: Woman, rather than Man. Once again, women and men are inherently different but inherently similar. This difference within likeness is the basis for their sexual relationship in a lifelong union: 'Therefore . . . they shall become one flesh' (v. 24). Procreation is not mentioned. The emphasis is rather on intimacy and companionship. Sexual difference is about more than fertility: there is something beautiful and significant in the encounter between woman and man.[14]

Deep intimacy and companionship can, of course, exist between people of the same sex – as Jesus himself shows. But whilst procreation is not essential to the 'one flesh' union of marriage, sexual difference is.[15] Once again,

---

[14]*Creation and Covenant*, p. 95.

[15]Not everyone understands 'one flesh' as a reference to sex, e.g. James V. Brownson, *Bible, Gender, Sexuality: Reframing the Church's Debate on Same-Sex Relationships*, (Grand Rapids, MI: Eerdmans, 2013), chapter 5. However, this is how Paul reads it in 1 Corinthians 6:16, as Brownson admits.

anyone who wishes to argue that sex must be within a life-long monogamous relationship but does not need to be between a woman and a man, needs to show why some features of the passage still apply today but not others.

Let's sum things up so far. Whilst there are two creation stories in Genesis 1 and 2, both stress sexual difference. God intended marriage to mean something, and sex within marriage has a particular and beautiful purpose. Sex isn't just a way to make babies, but a gift that brings husband and wife together into physical 'one flesh' union. This physical intimacy expresses and strengthens the bringing together of their lives. Sex has two purposes: procreation (emphasised by Gen. 1), and delight and intimacy between wife and husband (emphasised by Gen. 2). In both cases, the difference between men and women is essential, not accidental. This is why, whatever the excellent virtues of many same-sex relationships, and whatever the rights of providing them with legal protection and support, they cannot be regarded as marriage. Biblically speaking, sexual differentiation is inherent to marriage. And, if these relationships are good but not marriage, they cannot be the right place for sex. As we have seen, sex is an inherent part of marriage, and the Bible consistently regards sex as wrong when it takes place anywhere else.

Does the Bible ever prohibit same-sex activity directly?

As we've seen, there are good and particular theological reasons why sex is for marriage and why the nature of marriage is a lifelong union of one woman and one man. Having looked at these reasons, it is much easier to make sense of the texts which speak directly about same-sex activity. We can now read them within a coherent overall story that explains the rationale behind them.

First, a word about two biblical episodes that are *not* relevant. They are the very similar stories found in Genesis 19 and Judges 19. Both describe the men of a city (Sodom and Gibeah respectively) attempting to 'know' (i.e. have sex with) men who are staying the night as guests of an inhabitant of the city. In both cases, the host offers a woman or women to the crowd instead, and in Judges 19 the woman is abused so badly that she dies.

The reason that these two stories do not reflect on same-sex activity as such is that both cases involve attempted rape. Rape is wrong regardless of the sex of the victim in relation to their attacker, and the actions of the men of Sodom and Gibeah are just as repulsive to gay people as to anyone else. So whilst it is true that these passages clearly disapprove of the men of Sodom and Gibeah, it is misleading to suggest that this disapproval is relevant for thinking about loving and consensual same-sex intimacy.

Other verses, however, do comment on same-sex activity in much more general terms. Perhaps the most well known is Leviticus 18:22, 'You shall not lie with a male as with a woman; it is an abomination.'[16] This is a blanket prohibition of same-sex activity in general terms. However, a genuine question arises about whether this prohibition

---

[16]See also Leviticus 20:13.

should be taken to apply in all times and circumstances. The fact that something is in the Old Testament Law doesn't automatically mean it applies to us today. Few Christians today seek to live out every command in Leviticus literally. The use of this verse to rule out same-sex activity today has therefore been widely ridiculed.

Some of the Old Testament laws are what we might call moral commands, others govern the civil life of the people of Israel in their particular historical circumstances, and still others regulate their religious practices – circumcision, sacrifice, food laws and so on. The moral laws will always be binding (such as the commands not to murder and commit adultery). The historically conditioned civil laws are not literally binding on us, although we can learn from them (priests no longer inspect houses infected with mildew, but health and safety still matter). And, in the case of the religious laws, the New Testament often explicitly gives us reasons why we should no longer obey them. They are fulfilled in Christ and his 'once for all' sacrifice on the cross.

The debate arises, of course, because the Law does not come neatly colour-coded according to these categories. Some things in the wider passage of Leviticus 18 suggest that the prohibition on same-sex activity might be a temporary and religious rule. Many women and men might prefer not to have sex during the woman's period (v. 19), but few would consider it an absolute moral obligation. But apart from verse 19, all the other commands *do* seem to be permanent and moral, ruling out incest, adultery, child sacrifice and bestiality. So, whilst we cannot yet be

100 per cent sure that Leviticus 18:22 is a moral command that applies for all time, it is a strong possibility.

Whenever there is uncertainty about whether an Old Testament command still applies, it is worth asking what the New Testament says on the issue. I think that the New Testament makes it clear that the prohibition on same-sex activity is a permanent and binding one. Two passages are relevant.

The first is 1 Corinthians 6:9–10, in which Paul lists several types of people whom he says will not 'inherit the Kingdom of God', including the sexually immoral, idolaters, thieves, and the greedy. He cannot mean that if you have ever done any of these things, you have blown your chances forever, because he immediately adds, 'And such were some of you. But you were washed, you were sanctified, you were justified in the name of the Lord Jesus Christ and by the Spirit of our God' (v. 11). These sins are serious – but they do not get the last word.

Within the list, Paul uses two Greek words whose meanings have been heavily debated, *malakoi*, and *arsenokoitai* (which also occurs in 1 Tim. 1:9). *Malakoi* literally means 'soft ones.' This was pretty standard language for men who were the 'passive' partner in same-sex intercourse. *Arsenokoitai* is a combination of two other words: *arsen*, meaning 'man', and *koitos*, which means 'bed', but in a particularly sexual sense (it's where we get the word 'coitus' from). So, it's likely to be a reference to male same-sex intercourse, especially given its proximity to *malakoi*. Significantly, *arsen* and *koitos* both occur together in the Greek translation of the Old Testament, the Septuagint.

There, they are used to translate – guess what – Leviticus 18:22. So it seems pretty clear that Paul is here picking up the Old Testament prohibition of same-sex activity, and by using both *malakoi* and *arsenokoitai*, he is referring to both partners in male same-sex intercourse.

The second New Testament passage is Romans 1:26–28, which is the only place where same-sex desire (not just activity), and female homosexuality are mentioned. Paul wrote these verses in the middle of a long description of sin and its effects on humanity. The heart of sin is that humans (as a whole) 'suppress the truth' (v. 18) by wilfully ignoring the evident reality of God in creation (v. 20) and substituting idols for God. It is in this context that Paul says that 'women exchanged natural relations for those that are contrary to nature; and the men likewise gave up natural relations with women and were consumed with passion for one another' (vv. 26–27). Paul is not singling out these individuals for special criticism. Rather, he is saying that the existence of these desires is one of the consequences (not the only one – he mentions plenty of others) of humanity's general turning away from nature in order to ignore God. For Paul, it is so obviously 'contrary to nature' (v. 26) that it is for him an example of how far humanity has gone from the way God originally made us.

The words translated 'contrary to nature' (*para phusin* in Greek) have generated great debate. One argument is that 'nature' is not a reference to human nature as such, but the nature of that particular person, i.e. it refers to straight men who give up their straight nature to have sex with other men. Because we now (supposedly) know that there is a fixed, permanent gay orientation, this does not apply. Others suggest that the dominant types of same-sex activity at the time were prostitution and pederasty, and so these texts should not be taken to refer to permanent, consenting adult relationships.

I find these arguments highly unconvincing. They rely on reading Paul in the light of a particular modern interpretation of sexuality. And the fact is that there *were* adult, consenting same-sex relationships in the ancient world.[17] Paul's comments here don't suggest that same-sex activity is problematic because it is exploitative or abusive, but precisely because it involves two people of the same sex exchanging or giving up 'natural relations' with people of the opposite sex (vv. 26–27).

In conclusion, we have seen that the Old Testament contains a blanket prohibition of (male) same-sex activity. On its own, we can't tell for sure whether this was intended as a temporary legal or ceremonial command, or whether it expresses a permanent moral norm. But in the New Testament, at least two texts suggest that the prohibition is a permanent one. 1 Corinthians 6:9–10 uses the same language as the Greek version of Leviticus 18:22, and Romans 1 describes same-sex desire and activity (including between women) as 'contrary to nature'.

Plus, all this needs to be set in the context of the general biblical view (especially found in Genesis and in the

---

[17]See the article by Peter Ould in footnote 4 above, and Thomas K. Hubbard (ed.), *Homosexuality in Greece and Rome: A Sourcebook of Basic Documents* (Los Angeles, CA: University of California Press, 2003).

teaching of Jesus) that sex is a good gift for marriage, and that marriage is between a woman and a man. Given the strong emphasis in the Bible on female-male complementarity as an essential feature of marriage, the explicit prohibition of same-sex activity is exactly what we would expect to find. This complementarity is part of marriage for important and specific theological reasons.

It is not that the Bible singles out same-sex activity for more attention than any other sexual sin. It also rules out adultery, promiscuity, pre-marital sex, and so on. But these and same-sex activity are all ruled out for the same reason, namely that they involve sex taking place in a context other than the one it was made for: marriage between a woman and a man.

If two people love each other, why shouldn't they express that love through sex?

When the Gestapo arrested Dietrich Bonhoeffer, he was working on a book called *Ethics*. In it, he points out that Paul in 1 Corinthians 13 says that one can possess all manner of worthy characteristics (such as prophetic powers), do good deeds (give one's possessions to the poor), even undergo martyrdom – yet be without love.[18] This should make us pause before being too confident that we all know what love means.

Similarly, Bonhoeffer says, the verse 'God is love' (1 John 4:16) is persistently misread because we think that

---

[18]Dietrich Bonhoeffer, *Ethics*, tr. Ilse Tödt et al., ed. Eberhard Bethge et al. (Minneapolis, MN: Fortress, 2009), p. 332.

we understand the word 'love', and use that in order to understand God. Bonhoeffer thinks it should be the other way around: in order to understand love, we first need to know God.[19] God's love exists before our love and is the basis of our love: 'In this is love, not that we have loved God but that he loved us' (1 John 4:10). And the form that this takes is the cross of Christ: 'This is how we know what love is: Jesus Christ laid down his life for us' (1 John 3:16, NIV).

The argument that 'surely what matters is that two people love each other' is based on the human-centred understanding of love which Bonhoeffer criticises.[20] We should not infer the nature of love from people's experiences and feelings, if this means setting aside the theological significance of the difference between men and women as set out above. In other words, we need to understand love through Christian revelation, not through the human experience of love.

The reason for this is that human love, just like human everything else, is fallen. We cannot simply read off how we should act from how we feel. Our ability to observe

---

[19] *Ethics*, p. 334.

[20] Here is one example: 'Suppose two people loved each other with all their hearts, and they wanted to commit themselves to each other in the sight of God . . . to serve God together; to be faithful for the rest of their lives. If they were people of opposite sexes, we would call that holy and beautiful . . . But if we changed only one thing – the gender of one of those individuals – while still keeping the same love and selflessness and commitment, suddenly many Christians would call it abominable.' Justin Lee, *Unconditional: Rescuing the Gospel from the Gays-vs-Christians Debate* (London: Hodder & Stoughton, 2013), p. 185.

and think about ourselves is not fully reliable and our lives are fraught with self-deception. Plus we are no longer the way God originally intended us to be, in many respects. But the gospel and Jesus's teaching are clear.

Hence, even our love needs to be remade in the light of the cross and of Jesus's teaching. We must bring even our noblest and deepest feelings to Christ for him to revolutionise and transform them. As Paul puts it, love 'rejoices with the truth' (1 Cor. 13:6). We cannot know if love is love on its own. It needs the truth.

In my own case, it was precisely experiencing God's love that meant I did not simply go along with the pattern of my sexual feelings. It was God's love which led me to rejoice in the truth of my creation as a physically sexual being, which is what orders me towards either marriage or celibacy. The desire for a committed, sexually intimate relationship and the desire for intimacy with people of the same sex are not wrong desires. These desires are originally good and beautiful aspects of the way God has made us all. But for me, part of being fallen is that these two originally separate but good desires have been muddled up together. Therefore, I can't define love by my own perceptions or by how I feel. I have to look at who God says that I am. By not starting with my own experience of love, but letting myself be loved by God, I eventually came to an outcome that was not what I had expected at all, namely marriage.

Conclusion

I've tried to show here not only that Scripture rules out same-sex activity, which I think it does, but why.

We saw that Jesus's own view of sexual morality was founded on the creation stories in Genesis 1 and 2. By looking at those stories, we discovered that the classic Christian teaching on sex and marriage isn't a minor or peripheral theme within the biblical story. It is integral to central aspects of Christian faith, including Jesus's teaching about the nature of marriage, the Triune reality of God, the doctrine of union with Christ, the relationship between Christ and the church, and the goodness of human bodily existence. This is why when Scripture explicitly mentions same-sex activity, it does so in a 'consistently negative' way.[21]

Picture a woolly jumper with a loose thread sticking out. It looks messy and it spoils the whole jumper. So it's very tempting to yank the thread out. But when you pull it, instead of snapping, a bit more thread comes out with it. You could keep pulling, and pulling. More and more thread would keep coming out until the whole jumper was ruined because, at the end of the day, the jumper as a whole *is* thread.

The classic view of sexual morality is a bit like that. It seems inconvenient today. It's certainly unpopular. Some claim that it's putting gay people and others off church (although I actually doubt this claim). So, what could be simpler than to yank out and get rid of this unsightly and seemingly peripheral teaching? The problem is, as I hope I have shown, that this teaching is connected to many

---

[21]Christopher R. Seitz, *The Character of Christian Scripture* (Grand Rapids, MI: Baker Academic, 2011), pp. 176,178.

other things. If we yank out this teaching by saying that sometimes sex is OK outside marriage after all, we will have to find an alternative way of explaining why we still think that adultery and promiscuity are wrong. If we yank it out by expanding our definition of marriage beyond Jesus's definition of it as the one-flesh union of a woman and a man, then marriage will no longer be the wonderful picture of the gospel that it was intended to be. If sexual difference is not relevant for sexual union, even our account of God as Trinity, real difference within perfect union, is affected. If we keep pulling the thread, we may be shocked at how long it is, and how much of the jumper ends up coming out with it.

Go Deeper

For a very full discussion of the Bible and recent interpretations of it, see Martin Davie, *Studies on the Bible and Same-Sex Relationships since 2003* (Malton, N. Yorks: Gilead Books, 2015). A shorter Summary version is also available.

Lisa Diamond, 'Just How Different are Female and Male Sexual Orientation?' a lecture, online at http://www.cornell.edu/video/lisa-diamond-on-sexual-fluidity-of-men-and-women.

Christopher C. Roberts, *Creation and Covenant: The Significance of Sexual Difference in the Moral Theology of Marriage* (London: T & T Clark, 2007).

Jenell Williams Paris, *The End of Sexual Identity: Why Sex is Too Important to Define Who We Are* (Downers Grove, IL: IVP, 2011).

Why have so many Christians modernised their attitude to slavery and divorce, but not to homosexuality? Does this show that the church is homophobic?

- On slavery, see my article here: http://www.livingout.org/if-we-ve-rejected-what-the-bible-says-about-slavery-why-not-reject-what-it-says-about-homosexuality-too-.
- On divorce, see the companion study on divorce in my The Only Way is Ethics series.

ND - #0131 - 270225 - C0 - 198/129/2 - PB - 9781780781464 - Gloss Lamination